THE CHANGING

Kennington

BOOK TWO

Carole Newbigging

SERIES NUMBER 53

3302782463

Published by
Robert Boyd Publications
260 Colwell Drive
Witney, Oxfordshire OX28 5LW

First published 2002

Copyright © Carole Newbigging
and *Robert Boyd Publications*

ISBN: 1 899536 64 7

Printed and bound in Great Britain at
The Alden Press, Oxford

TITLES IN THE *CHANGING FACES* SERIES

Contents

Cover Illustrations

Front: Mike Clark outside the VG Store, on the corner of Kenville Road

Back: The Scholar Gipsy football team c1992 at Playfield Road recreation ground.

Left to right back row: Geoff Dighton, Gary Dighton, Andy Gill, Nigel Cattell, Shaun Lydon, Steve Elwood, Terry Mathews, Ray Brown. *Front row:* Chris Ledger, Stuart Giles, Neil Johnson, Alex Crossan, Kevin Herridge, Steve Moncur, Gregg Parrott

Acknowledgements

Kennington is fortunate in having an excellent collection of material, through the efforts of the Kennington History Project. It is with grateful thanks that I acknowledge this collection, which has provided much of the factual information contained within this book. The Collection contains records of personal memories from various dates, and these have been invaluable in giving an eye-witness account of life in Kennington throughout the years. I also acknowledge assistance received from the photographic library of the Oxford Mail and Times.

I would particularly thank the following individuals who have kindly allowed me to use their own photographs and material Mr and Mrs Bennett, Pete and Margaret Biggs, Mrs Anne Box, Liz Brookes, Clive Calver, Eric Clarke, Mrs K Clarke, Mike and Jane Clarke, Mr Deane, David Eggleton, Doug and Ruby Francis, Cliff and Vera Godfrey, Jane Greig, Audrey Hartigan, Mrs P Hill, Glenys Hookham, Mrs Irene Hosking, Ken Johnson, Shirley and Idris Jones, Joy Ledger, Kate Mingham, Dennis Murray, Rear-Admiral J A L Myres, Pat O'Reilly, Mr and Mrs Peter Peace, June Poole, Maureen Pope, Mr Raworth, Sylvia Rivers, Eileen Rodgers, George and Carole Ross, Gerald Shayler, Doreen Smith, Pat Smith, Dennis and Kathleen Tasker, Tony and Rose Taylor, George and Betty Trinder, Judy Vause, Sylvia Vetta, Mrs Beryl Walters, Muriel Woodruff, Mrs Gladys Wyatt – and the many more residents, past and present, who have given freely of their time providing information and helping to identify photographs.

Finally, I would apologise to anyone whom I have inadvertently omitted to thank, and those who have, despite best efforts, remain unidentified, or wrongly identified, within these pages. All names, facts and dates are subject to human memory and errors do, inevitably, creep in.

It is hoped this second book will complement the material in Kennington Book I and continue to give an insight into the development and history of Kennington.

Schools

Kennington school in 1904. The teacher on the far left was Winifred Irene Davis. Miss Davis was born in Speedwell Street, Oxford, in March 1889, the daughter of George and Rachel Ann Davis. Rachel Ann was headmistress of St Aldates School during the 1890s, retiring in 1895. George and Rachel Ann ran the Cross Keys public house in South Hinksey from about 1897 to 1930. Their daughter Winifred also went into teaching, and was at Kennington School from 1904, leaving to become a nurse. She married Daniel Jarman of South Street, Osney, in 1914.

Kennington School in 1926.

A nativity play at Kennington School in 1956 – How Far Is It to Bethlehem. During this time the reception class and first years were situated in the Village Hall, while the two storey block at the Junior School was built. By 1958 these classes had returned to the main school buildings.

A class in 1957 at the Village Hall, with teacher Mrs Brenda Cowlett. Left to right back row: Nigel Canning, Sally Duffy, David Jacques, Odette Holt, Robert Johnson, Ann Rosser, Steven Hanks, Katherine Shayler, Tony Buckle, Diana Todd, Steven Bloomfield. Middle row: Alan Bennell, Kathryn Ashton, Carol Evans, Gillian Hagen, Janet Tomlin, Mary Ann Bloomfield, Katherine Field, Anita James, Maureen Legge, Tony Day. Front row: Andrew -, Clive Brooks, Raymond Talbot, Robert Betteridge, Nigel Goodey, Tony Rivers, David Shelton, Alex Neve, Robert Hunt, Jonathan Vigor.

1960 left to right back row: Philip Walkington, David Villabois, Ann Rosser, Richard Field, Marianne Eldridge, Neville Westlake, Robin Cox teacher at the back, Wendy Villabois, Martin Tasker, Sandra Canning?, David Hartigan, Valerie Peedle, Andrew Bolt, Richard Field. Middle row: Jeanette Heggerty?, Ann Barnes, Cynthia Lucas, Rosemary-, -, Mrs Gorvett?, -, Ann Thomlin, Rosemary-, -, Nicola Smith? Front row: David Handley?, -, Bernard Workman, -Brookes, Rodney Gidding, Bobby Hamlet, Chris Thompson, Paul Orr, Tony Rivers, Chris Casson, -, Malcolm Caddick.

1961 left to right back row: Helen Woods, Christine Grant-Robertson, Diana Thorpe, Janet Whitehouse, Susan Kirby, Pauline Cox, Hilary Perkins, Kathleen Sharpe. Next row: David Taylor, Stuart Almond, Oliver Sutton, Paul Woodruff, Paul Swan, Lincoln Fishpool, Robert Drewsden, Chris Amor, Neil Hartigan, Derek Rogers, Russell Hallam. Next row: Angela Mills, Judith Ainsley, Jane Goodey, Miss East teacher, Penelope Townsend, Jane House, Doreen Lovett. Front row: Clive Harold, Peter Kubat, Adam Bishop, Kelvin Jones, Victor Morris, Keith Ware, Martin Pether, Keith Richards, Andy Barnes.

1960 Kennington School Football Team. Left to right back row: Philip Walkington, David Hartigan, Dean Bonner?, Andrew Bolt, Stephen Hanks, David Villabois, Richard Field. Front row: Nigel Goodey, Bobby Hamlet, Eric Field, Chris Thompson, Paul Swanson.

1963 left to right back row: Susan Vaughan, Tom Rosser, Janet Whitehouse, Susan Kirby, Christine Grant-Robertson, Diana Thorpe, Helen Woods. Next row: Graham Canning, Robert Drewsden, Paul Swan, Lincoln Fishpool, Oliver Sutton, Mark Lemon, Russell Hallam, Chris Amor, Derek Rogers, Peter Knight, John Hamlet. Next row: Pauline Cox, Hilary Perkins, Penelope Townsend, Jane House, Mrs Brenda Cowlett teacher, Susan Archer, Angela Mills, Jane Goodey, Doreen Lovett, Judith Ainsley. Front row: Martin Pether, David Taylor, Stuart Almond, Neil Hartigan, Clive Harold, Adam Bishop, Keith Ware, Victor Morris, Derek Wadson, Keith Richards.

1964 left to right back row: Stella Evans, Nicholas Lemmon, Angela Baker, Peter Chetnik, Janet Naish, Alan Crowder, Marianne Thompson, Andrew Massingham, Joanne Millard, Edward Clemence, Gillian Griffin, Philip Collis, Annette Rybar, Martin Adams. Next row: Michelle Collins, Francis Drake, Pamela Maynard, Shirley Harris, Elizabeth Metcalf, Miss Jenkins, Elizabeth Finch, Karen Rogers, Susan Cousins, Jennifer Hitchen, Sarah Egglestaff. Front row: Keith Hunt, David Eggleton, David Crossley, Adrian Ware, Sean Mills, Kim Dixie, Timothy Hallam, Stuart Giles, Paul Pratley, Mark Whittingham, Nicholas Winning, Robert Ferriman.

1962 Mrs Gorvette's class. Left to right back row: Katherine Field, Elizabeth Tucker, Katherine Shayler, Odette Holt, Kathryn Ashton, Janet Tomlin, Maureen Legge, Elaine Bayliss. Next row: Carol Rawlings, Annette Gower, Bruce Bignall, Steven Hanks, Dean Bonner, Steven Haw(?), Martin Simpson, Michael Kentfield, Ian Grant Robertson, John Thompson, Kathleen Field. Next row: Gillian Patterson, Julie Horwood, Margaret Godfrey, Linda Grace, Angela Smith, Anne Knight, Linda Bellerby, Sharon Finlay, Susan Wiggins. Front row: Andrew Wild, Nigel Goodie, Paul Swanson, Roderick Ball, Kenneth Blair, Nicholas Goodall, Nicholas Sharp, Jonathan Vigor.

1966 with Mrs Peart. Left to right back row: Mark Swanson, Paul Bennett, Peter Pratley, Diane Thomson, Simon Holloway, Claire Williamson, John Brophy, Martin MacMarne, Nicola Cummings, Philip Ashton, Anola Smith, Paul Gledhill, Raymond Smith, David Swanson. Middle row: Mark Stephens, Pauline Waistie, Zoe Davis, Jacqueline King, Alison Jones, Caroline Kitson, Carole Walker, Clare Hookham, Jane Massingham, Elaine Brooks, Marion Adams, Paul Appleton. Front row: Michael Boyne, David Richards, Christopher Druce, Christopher Tolley, Philip Sumpter, Melvin Summersbee, Desmond Harris, Kieron Donague, Paul Crookes, Dean Cummingham.

1958 Mrs Peart's class. Left to right back row: Robert Hunt, Katherine Shayler, David Crozier, Sally Duffy, David Gates, Odette Holt, Stephen Hanks, Kathryn Ashton, Tony Buckle. Middle row: Robert Betteridge, Diana Todd, Phillipa Smith, Maureen Legge, Carol Evans, Raymond Talbot. Front row: Andrew Sinclair Day, Ian Grant Robertson, Alex Neve, Stephen Bloomfield, Martin Simpson, Paul Canning, Paul Swanson, Nigel Goodey, Jonathan Vigor, Tony Day.

Mrs Gledhill's class c1966. Left to right back row: Margaret Cox, Colin Brandish, Suzanne Mattheson, Alan Hill, Karen James, Kevin Dean, Jackie Hudson, Graeme Laidler, Penelope Winning, Roy Tomlin?, Deborah Butler, Richard Griffin, -. Middle row: Beverley Griffin, Janet Belcher, Sally Woodley, Debbie Green, -, Mrs Gledhill, Karen Ware, Mandy Goodey, Anne Ledger, Toni Heath, Beatrix Taylor, -. Front row: Claudio Grendli, Paul Hamlett, Paul Dixey, Michael Ibbott, Alan Baker, Richard Francis?, -, Alan Franklin, -, Stephen-, -, Neil Scott, Stephen Glover.

1967 Mrs Shepherd's class. Left to right back row: Anola Smith, Simon Holloway, Graham Tolley, Philip Ashton, Clare Hookham, John Brophy, Claire Williamson, Martin MacMarne, Nicola Cummings, Malcolm Gibbs, Paul Appleton, Peter Pratley, Raymond Smith, Jacqueline King. Middle row: Elaine Brooks, Carolyn Paul, Caroline Kidson, Zoe Davis, Carole Walker, Alison Jones, Jane Massingham, Diane Thompson, Marion Adams, Pauline Waistie. Front row: Philip Sumpter, Mark Swanson, Mark Stephens, Paul Bennett, Dean Cunningham, Melvin Summersbee, Kieron Donague, David Swanson, Christopher Druce, Desmond Harris, Paul Crooks, Michael Boyne.

July 1981 and the children of St Swithun's say goodbye to Mr Arthur Newall, their headmaster for the past sixteen years. Pupils Vincent Becket and Ruth Bishop are pictured presenting a plant to Mr Newall on behalf of all the children.

Chairman of the Parish Council, Mrs Hettie Perkins, presents a chess set to St Swithun's School's Young Players in 1983. The large wooden-framed board, engraved with the school name and its string of competition successes was presented by Kennington Parish Council in recognition of the school's achievement in winning the county primary schools' championships in addition to the county under 11 league for the past three years. The chess club was started by teacher, John Walker.

St Swithuns School Playgroup in 1989. Left to right back row: Shona-, Lesley Holiday, Kian Rackley, Barry Graves, Clare Battle, Zara Beech, Oliver Mingham, Barbara Granahan, Trisha Mundy. Next row: Nina Anderson, Georgina Olley, Matthew Rylett, Lewis Gosling, Hayley Kirby, Toby Brown, Mark Kelleher, Andrew-, Selina Audit. Next row: Lucy Wilson, Paul Collins, David Grabham, Madiha Khan, Amy Breakspear, Lauren-, Sarah Keene, Christopher-, Tim Marshall. Front row: Jordan Halsey, Mathew-, Alistair Jones, Luke Hulewicz, Philip Wicker, Emma Jane Greig, Emma Bowler, Nicola Burton, Robert-, Rebecca Andrews, David Guest.

St Swithuns Rowan Class of 1989. Left to right back row: Mrs Lord, Alastair Robbins, Fay Biggadike, Clara Jones, Louise Russell, Frances Henley, Chris White, Hailey Latsch. Next row: Hissam Khan, Claire Eggleton, Ashley Smith, Aaron Webster, Mathew Tomkins, Zoe Thomas, Hannah Revell, Ben Spiers. Next row: Iain Greig, Richard Francis, Rosalind Craven, Nicholas Himpson, Melanie Willi, David Bushen, Steven Hartigan. Front row: Catherine Guest, Elizabeth Rhymes.

School Nativity Play c1964

Oak Class at St Swithin's School celebrates the school centenary in 1990, when the children and staff dressed up in 19th century dress. Left to right back row: Derek Matthews, Adam Hulewicz, Tom Olley, Daniel Morris, Michael Norburn, Caroline Marshall, Lucy Fletcher, Leanne Mingham. Front row: James Morris, Vincent Davidson, -, Clements?, Billy Beck, Mr Allcock headteacher, Mrs Hill teacher, Jenny Young, Clare Battle, Abigail New, Erin Mutton, Natalie Element.

Children from Kennington School at the production of 'Oliver' in May 1994, one of the many school musicals produced by Miss Jane Eddie.Left to right back row: Katie Winchester, Melanie Cobb, Cressida Kirtland, Daniel Morris, Ollie Carter, Carl Hewlett, Adam Bowler. Next row: Olivier Jones, Sophie Brown, Leanne Mingham, Claire Atkinson. Front row: Richard Francis, Zoe Thomas, Matthew Robbins, Daniel Forder.

Kennington School Athletic Team during an inter-school competition at Horspath Road, c1983. Left to right back row: Mathew Webb, Ben Harding, Paul Slade, James Warner, David Ross, Kevin Hickman. Front row: Heide Rolfe, -, -, -, Lindsay Smith, -, -.

St Swithuns Infants School – originally called Underwoods. This photograph was taken c1973 after a production of 'The Pied Piper of Hamlyn'. Left to right back row: Jenny Osbourn, Caroline Jenkins, Sonia -, Deborah Prince, Ben Vause. Middle row: Simon Troth, Nicola Avery, Paul Simpson, Stephen Everett, -, Nicholas Westbury, David Anders. Front row: Verity -, Louise Elston, Geoffrey Cox, Jane Bowley, Sally Ross, Justine Clarke, Yvone Shayler, Amanda Warwick. The school was eventually amalgamated with St Swithun's Junior School in the late 1980s.

Underwood's staff in the 1970s. Left to right back row: Ruth Hooper, Jean Evans, Mr Evans, Sylvia Egglestaff, Bob Vause, Mr Gledhill, Mr Egglestaff, Mr Davies. Front row: Marjorie Gledhill, Judy Vause, Irene Rowden, Mr Underwood caretaker, Barbara Boyne, Gwladys Davies headteacher. *'The children thought the school was named after Mr Underwood, our caretaker, but I think it was named because of its proximity to Bagley Woods.'*

Underwood's staff in the early 1980s. Left to right back row: Elaine Spires, Les Tappin caretaker, Beryl Hamlet dinnerlady, Betty Goodenough cook. Front row: Liz Trevett secretary, Barbara Boyne, Gwladys Davies headteacher, Judy Vause, Ruth Hooper.

Kennington and its People

Village Hall group taken c1950. The hall was used to hold whist drives and parties to raise funds for old folk in Kennington. Back row left to right: Mrs Ellen Brooks, Mrs Acott, Miss Back, -. Middle row: Mrs Pope, -, Phyllis Westbrook, Mrs Gladys Wyatt, -, Sid Acott, Mrs Prior, Miss Gladys Palmer, George Simpson, Mrs Elsie Blakeman, Mrs Simpson. Front row: Mrs Edie Peedell, Mrs Butler.

Bonfire site at the top of Poplar Grove c1947. Left to right: Neville Bell, John Launchbury, Graham Pitts. In front: Tony Simms. The bonfire was an annual event and was always lit by Ted Nash. The flat roofed building behind the bonfire was the Cold Store – now the site of Otters Reach.

Left to right: Pete Woodley, Bob Purvey, Brian Clarke, Jennifer Nash c1947 at the top of Poplar Grove.

This photograph taken during the 1940s is of Mrs Doris Baskerville of No 5 Poplar Grove on the left with Mrs Doris Clarke of No 3 Poplar Grove on the right.

Denise Kirby from No 7 Poplar Grove, Pete Woodley, Johnny Grant, Geoff Nash, Marlene Lovett and Brian Clarke, taken on Brian's birthday c1955 at No 3 Poplar Grove.

This bungalow, No 150 Kennington Road, was occupied by Mr and Mrs Frederick Stayt during the 1950s. Mrs Stayt was instrumental in introducing the Young People's Fellowship to Kennington. The building was laid right off the Kennington Road, behind the post office, towards Oxford. There are now two large houses on this site. The front garden was very long and full of vegetables.

Mrs Stayt at Edith Court in the 1980s, visited by Dennis Murray. Mrs Stayt is remembered as being very religious with *'a lovely face, she must have been very beautiful when young'*.

Horace and Edith Walker lived in The Rosary (now 38 Kennington Road) in the 1920s. During this time Horace built, completely by himself, the house called 'Sherwood' at 31 Upper Road and the family moved in 1929. This house had oak panelling and an oak staircase. Mr Walker sold a plot of land next door Mr Bill Gray, manager of Forest Side Nursery, who had two semi-detached houses built, one he lived in and the other he sold to Mr Alf Sherwin.

'Sherwood' 31 Upper Road c1929.

Horace and Edith Walker in 1961

1947 wedding at the old St Swithin's church, of Mr and Mrs Walkers daughter, Doreen, to Bill Smith.

Mr Horace Walker in 1948 with his grandson, Rodney, and family friend Joan Gray, daughter of neighbour Bill Gray.

Left to right: Cliff Godfrey, Les Jackman, Dick Godfrey and George Trinder, in 1948 leaning against Ray Chasney's taxi, outside the Tandem public house.

At the back is Johnny Keep, local builder, on left Gerald Shayler and on right George Trinder, both local postmen. This photograph was taken at the time the post office was being extended in 1969.

August 1949 in front of the Tandem garages. Left to right: Jeannie James, Brian Giles, Norman Chasney, Jean Pontin. The rail in front of these garages was a popular meeting place. The building is still standing, to the left of the Tandem, now used as a store.

In front of the social club, the Working Mens' Club, in July 1947. Left to right: Dickie Godfrey, Arthur Berry, George Gunn, George Trinder – all just demobbed from the army.

An outing from the Tandem in 1947. Left to right back row: Bryn Giles, Vera Smewin, Bill Pitter, Betty Pitter, Dickie Godfrey, George Trinder, -, Bill Davis. In front: Margaret Hodnett, Daphne Wacknell, Rosie Godfrey, Dick Wacknell (middle), Norman Chasney, Les Wacknell. To the right of the group are 'Son' Earles and Rosemary Pitter.

Commendation Certificate awarded in 1944 to John Cyril Smewin, signalman, for averting a potentially disastrous rail accident on the railway line at Kennington.

John Cyril Smewin, known as Curly, was born at 'Norfolk Cottage' in Radley in 1891. He, and his five brothers and one sister, travelled by horse and cart to Kennington School. He joined the Great Western railway, firstly as a porter at Radley Station, but later as a signalman at Nuneham Courteney, before becoming signalman at Kennington Station. He died in 1956, only three months after his retirement.

1951 photograph of the Smewin family. Left to right: Joe, Maud, Fred, Will, Cyril, Edgar, George. Several of Cyril's brothers were also involved with the railway: Joe was an engine driver, Fred a station master at Bristol, Will lived at 73 Kennington Road and was an inspector at Oxford station, Edgar also worked at Oxford station, George lived at 49 Kennington Road. His sister, Maud, married a signalman from Abingdon station.

Charles St Swithun Villebois, born 1888, and his wife Mabel, outside their cottage in Bagley Wood Road in the 1920s when they were first married.

After five years or so, they moved to one of the cottages 'down the dip' opposite the present day co-operative shop. After briefly moving to Upper Road the family returned to the same cottage in Kennington Road, where they remained until the cottages were condemned in 1946, at which time they moved to the newly built 30 Poplar Grove. Mr Villebois died a few months before his 91st birthday.

At the end of the 19th century an Oxford lady, Mrs Mary Rowley, wife of one of the early missionaries to Central Africa, had an accident when driving through Kennington in her pony carriage. She was so impressed with the kind hospitality offered her by the people of Kennington that she retained an interest in the village and its people.

Mary Rowley's first godchild was Charles St Swithun Villebois, who was born in 1888. His second name, St Swithun, reflected her interest in the Kennington church. Mrs Rowley died in 1900 and a few months later, at the age of 12, Charles followed his father into agriculture. In December 1914 he entered war service, and was badly wounded at the Somme. In 1917 he was gassed at Cambrai and was sent home. He worked at Radley College as a gardener, but later moved to Morris Motors and then the Cowley Concrete Company. For the last twenty years of working life he was gateman at the cold storage depot, now the site of Otters Reach. He retired in 1958 at the age of 70.

The Oxford University Golf Club – Cranbrook House

Charles Sanders Raworth was born in Bridgewater, Somerset in 1876 and married Amelia Jane Wigmore of South Hinksey in April 1901, her family owning a farm there as part of Wigmore dairies. The family lived in St Aldates, then in Grandpont Villas on the Abingdon Road, before moving to the old Oxford University Golf Club House at Kennington about 1921. This photograph was taken c1921. Left to right back row: Gwendolen Rayworth, who married Harold Poole of St Aldates and Marjorie Raworth who married Hector Spinks, a local Kennington family. Middle row: Mrs Amelia Jane Raworth, Leonard, known as Bill, who married Nora Webber, Charles Sanders Raworth. Front row: Mabel who married Philip Griston of North Walsham in Norfolk and Vernon Raworth who died of diptheria at 5 years old.

Charles Raworth was well known for his love of gardening and particularly enjoyed growing onions, tomatoes and roses. Mr Raworth died in 1959 and his widow moved to live with her daughter, Gwendolen. The property was sold to local builder, Mr R D Davies, and family, who remain in the property.

Cranbrook House c1929. The Oxford University Golf House was renamed by Charles Raworth as Cranbrook House, after the Canadian town of Cranbrook, where his brothers Arnold and Archibald had set up a jewellery business after emigrating. Charles ran the coachbuilding business of Charles Raworth & Son Limited in St Aldates, Oxford. The company had close links with Morris Motors of Cowley and car chassis were delivered from Morris's for Raworths to complete the building of the car bodies.

A photograph of the interior c1920s. This was referred to as the Big Room, and contained a billiard table. Across the back wall can be seen the original lockers used by members of the Golf Club.

The pool that used to be at the front of the house, bordering the main road.

Another view of Cranbrook House during the 1930s.

'I remember Mr Raworth's house quite well. At that time there were no other buildings between his house and Bagley Wood; we always referred to the area around his house as the 'golf links' because that's exactly what it was at one time. He had, I believe, an artisan well in the garden and the pump was driven by a windmill. Carol singing at Christmas was very popular in those days, and each Christmas a group of five or six of us would make a special point of trekking up to the Raworth house to give our rendering. I used to play the mouthorgan and accompany the singing and we would go to the side entrance and sing properly; no knocking on the door or messing about. If Mrs Raworth came to the door, she would leave the door open and fetch Mr Raworth and they would usually request a carol or two. There would be at least 2sh 6d put in our money box and we would come away with oranges, mince pies etc.'

St Swithun's House, 218 Kennington Road

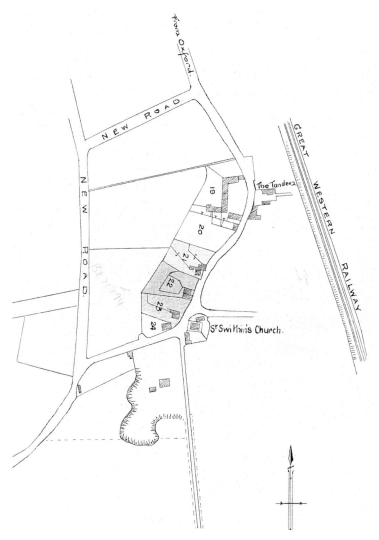

The three plots of land - numbered 21, 22 and 23 – were sold by Edgar Norton Disney to Arthur Millin, tailor of 17 Edith Road Oxford on 5 August 1913. The prices paid for the plots were £145 for plot 21, £160 for plot 22 and £175 for plot 23 – a total of £480 for an area of '1 acre, 1 rood and 21 poles'. The land contained 8 cottages, respectively occupied by Richard Gibbons, Mrs Greenaway and Mrs Steptoe (plot 21), two owned by Mrs Munday with a third one vacant (plot 22), and, lastly, Mr G Gibbons and J Villabois (plot 23).

In 1920 Arthur Millin sold most of this land to William Ellis Cotton, tobacconist of 18 Turl Street, for the sum of £675. Cotton in turn sold to Frank John Tindall Jones of Bryher, 167 Kennington Road, a mineral water manufacturer, for the sum of £800. In 1924 a mortgage document refers to two tenements formerly two semi-detached tenements erected thereon and now known as 'Saint Swithuns'.

St Swithun's House in 1913

Frank Jones died on 6 April 1944 and his widow Florence Kathleen Jones, ran an antique business from the house. She died at St Swithuns on 9 March 1954. The property was inherited by her niece, Ivy Kathleen Shrimpton, wife of William Ewert Shrimpton, teacher. On 22 September 1967 Mrs Shrimpton sold the property for £7,300 to Frank Hales, a local government officer of 31 The Avenue. On his death the property was inherited by his daughter, Anne Hales.

No 96 Kennington Road – Fairfield – in 1960, prior to alterations. This house was built in 1910, but not completed until 1912. In 1913 it was occupied by William Chamberlain, and by Frederick Young in 1921. By 1925 the occupant was a gentleman by the name of Thynne, but occupied by Joseph King in 1937 and 1939. Since 1960 it has been the property of Dr Christopher Strode.

No 1 Cow Lane c1908. This cottage was occupied by Mr and Mrs Godfrey, one of several Godfrey families living in Kennington at that time. The Godfrey family, Jimmy born in 1894 and sisters, Emie, Hilda, Florrie, Nellie and Polly, were all born in this cottage. The family later moved to a cottage where 216 Kennington Road is now situated. Neither of these cottages now exist. Jimmy married Rosalie Morbey in 1921 and moved to, what was then, No 1 Upper Road, one of the St John's College cottages built to accommodate Bagley Wood employees. Jimmy worked at Bagley Wood until he was 80 years old, and died in 1987 at the age of 93. A memorial stone in Bagley Wood was erected in his memory. (This is a correction to Book 1).

One of the Godfrey sisters, Hilda on the left, in the river at Sandford with Jackie Peedell, Clifford Godfrey, Dick Godfrey and Cyril Peedell, c1930. Another Godfrey sister, Polly, had married Jack Peedell and lived at 'Bryher' 167 Kennington Road with sons, Jackie and Cyril.

Clifford Godfrey, Richard Godfrey and Arthur Berry c1930.

Jimmy Godfrey with sons, Richard and Clifford, c1928 at 1 Upper Road, one of the Woodmen's Cottages, built in 1922. The haystack lay next to the cottage, where the lane now leads into Templeton Cottage.

Deeds to the house show it was leased, in December 1911, by Edgar Norton Disney to Sergeant Charles Edward Thomas Richmond, builder of 56 Argyle Street, Oxford. The property at that time was approximately 1 acre, having a frontage of 100ft and depth of 436ft. In 1914 Richmond was apparently a Sgt Major in the Royal Army Medical Corps, serving with the British Expeditionary Force. On 10 March 1919 Sgt Major Richmond assigned the leasehold to Mr Bernard Smallbone of Newlyn, Wantage Road, Didcot, signalman on the Great Western Railway. At that time the property is referred to as Gibraltar House. Mr Smallbone purchased the freehold in 1928 for the sum of £150. When he died on 19 October 1962, Mr Smallbone left the house to Mrs Dorothy Cooke of Bagley Wood Lodge, wife of Albert William Cooke. It is believed that Mrs Cooke was his housekeeper. The executor of the Will was Mr Eric Keith Fisher, railway clerk of Earley near Reading, and nephew of Mr Smallbone. The property remained empty until sold for £4,700 to Dr and Mrs Barrie E Juniper in August 1964.

Gibraltar House, 53 Little London (Bagley Wood Road)

Mr Tony Bennett outside 29 Kennington Road. This property was built in 1928 for Mr James Bennett, cabinet maker, and his wife Violet, who moved to Kennington from St Ebbes. Their only son, Mr Tony Bennett, inherited the bungalow when his father died in 1982. He started to keep chickens in the early 1950s, and has always enjoyed keeping geese as pets because they 'are more intelligent'.

Pete Biggs of Grundy Crescent, cutting the grass next to the war memorial in 2000. Pete and Margaret Biggs have always been active in village life, and Pete has been chair of the Parish Council for many years. Margaret, a registered nurse, has maintained a lifelong interest in guides, and both have been involved in the Kennington Amateur Dramatic Society.

Dr Geoffrey Blackman. *'If anyone could be said to be the most loved and respected man in the village it was Dr Blackman, for many years the only doctor in the village until joined by Dr Strode. He didn't have an appointment system, but you took you turn, and he saw everyone who came, no matter what the time. It didn't matter how many people were waiting – when it was your turn you were the only one who mattered. He would sit by his desk, slippers on, listening to you, cleaning, filling and lighting his pipe, although he never smoked it. It made you relax. He must have been exhausted most evenings. Nothing was ever too much trouble. He died far too soon after his retirement, and he was mourned throughout the village'.*

George and Carole Ross moved to Kennington in 1976 and George served as clerk to the Parish Council for more than 25 years, retiring in July 2002. Carole helped with the administration as assistant clerk. In recognition of their service, part of an area developed on the site of the Scholar Gipsy public house has been named Ross Court.

Kennington has a long tradition of paying tribute to key community figures by naming streets and roads after them. Previous tributes include Simpsons Way after George Simpson first chairman of Kennington Parish Council in 1936; Perkins after Ted Perkins Chairman of the Parish Council for 12 years until 1974; Liddiard Close after The Rev. Thomas Hearne Liddiard Kennington vicar from 1937 to 1946; Grundy Crescent after Mr Samual Percy Grundy, Rural District Councillor and Chairman of the Parish Council in the 1940s; and Kirk Close after George Kirk council member from 1940 to 1952; and Blackman Close after Dr Geoffrey Blackman.

SECTION THREE

Organisations

The 1925 banner of the Women's Institute

Below:Kennington Women's Institute in the 1930s. The WI was started in Kennington in 1925 and continues to the present day.

Left to right back row: Mrs Wyatt, Mrs Acaster, Mrs Baskerville, Mrs Pitter, Mrs Clark of 3 Poplar Grove, Miss W Back, Miss Westbrooke, -, Mrs Humpreys, Mrs R Nash, Mrs Blakeman, Mrs G Farr, Miss P Westbrook, Mrs N Pitts, Doris Powell, Mrs Horn, -, Miss Blunson, -, Mrs Faulkner (post mistress), -, -, Mrs Underwood, Mrs Gale. Middle row: Mrs Walker, Mrs Wallis, Mrs Wheeler, Mrs Broomfield, -, Mrs J Butterfield, -, Miss Wigmore, Mrs S Tomline, Mrs Ball, Mrs D Kerby, Miss Rockall, -, Mrs Walters, Mrs Wichall, -, Mrs W Gobey, Mrs Bucknell, Mrs Avery, Mrs Gerrard, -, -, Mrs George Simpson, Mrs Butler.   Front row: Miss Brown, Mrs Spracklen, Mrs Palmer, Mrs Tombs, Mrs Francis, Mr Theobald, Mrs Kerby, Mrs Acott, Miss Trevellyan, Mrs Evers, Mrs Rowles, Miss E Davenport (president), Mrs Mills, Mrs Finch, -, -, Mrs Arkell, Mrs Ayliffe, Mrs Coggan.

Kennington Overseas Aid Week 1 July 1972, and pony rides were a popular fundraising event. Left to right: -, Mary Chasney, Jane Amor, Sally Chasney. (Photograph: David Green)

1 July 1972, this delightful monster (the vicarage hedge dressed up) faced the main entrance and challenged all-comers to guess his name. Nobody did. It was 'The Bhola Bug' - Bhola Island in Bangladesh being supported by Kennington Overseas Aid that year. (Photograph: David Green)

In 1967, Rose Taylor, a member of the Good Shepherd Church, together with the Reverend Davis encouraged all the village churches to unite, in an organisation called 'the people next door'. From this started the Kennington Good Neighbours and Overseas Aid. The Kennington Christian Service Group was formed in April 1968, with a committee responsible for organizing the Good Neighbours Scheme. The first project to benefit from Kennington Overseas Aid week – from 15 to 21 June 1969 - was the village of Otterthotti in Madras, South India, which received £60 towards the construction of dams and wells. The following year the committee set a target of £500 for leprosy relief in Malawi. The week of activities raised £1,150 – well in excess of anyone's expectations.

Kennington Youth Band was formed by Ron Sudworth as a break-away from the City of Oxford Silver Band. An inaugural meeting c1979 was held in the garden of Peter Hooper's house, at 143 Upper Road. Left to right back row: Simon Turnbull, -, Martin Sudworth, Clifford Sadler, Martin Ferriman, -, -Sudworth, -, Ron Sudworth, Adrian Pope, Margaret Cox, Caroline Gardiner?, -, Claire Tritton, Linda Raye, -, Mark Hooper.   Middle row: -, Stewart Black, Gary Collins, Amanda Black, David Clack, Chris Munt, Stuart Collins.   Front row: -Hooper, -, -, -, -, Karen-.

The first Kennington Players in a production of Cinderella in 1946. Left to right back row: Eileen Tiffin, Joan Wheal, Esther Goddard, Les Thompson, -, Eva Elston, Sylvia Theobald, Mrs Tiffin, Arthur Lord, Beryl Kimber, Marjorie Woodward, -.   Middle row: -, Shirley Moffett, Sally Underwood, -, Shirley Tiffin, Margaret Thomas, Jackie Howard, Margaret Beyer, -, Mrs Rowles.   Front row: Esme Howard?, Sally Williamson, Beryl Reid, Janet Theobald, Andrina Walker, Gillian Wyatt, Bobby Wheal, Pamela Hewer, Gwenda Hughes?.

Kennington Players' production of Robin Hood during the 1940s – possibly in the grounds of St Veeps, Bagley Wood Road. Group includes Mrs Elston 4th from left, 'Johnnie' Kirby kneeling, and Sylvia Francis 7th from left.

Mr Charles Minchin, on the left, with Mr Lord in a Kennington Players Revue about 1950. Kennington Players finished in the 1950s and was resurrected in February 1979 as KADS – Kennington Amateur Dramatic Society. Mr Minchin ran a grocery shop at 19 The Avenue, between the Scholar Gipsy public house and the garage, later run by Mr Hurcombe. The property is now two houses.

'Son of Ali Baba' or — The Beggers of Bagley Wood

CAST

Chota Baba	(son of Ali Baba)	David Goldsworthy
Camelia	(his camel)	Antoinetta Graves & George Ross
Morgani	(Chota's lost fiancee)	Annette Barrett
Cousin Hussein (Son of Cassim, Ali Baba's brother)		Atam Vetta
Mora Dis	(Hussein's wife)	Johnnie Kirby
Lessa Dat	(Hussein's mother)	Philip Martin

The daughters of Hussein and Mora Dis

Sheil	Helen Biggs
Bet	Sally Ross
Sonia	Rebecca Martin
Notta	Imelda Bye
Yessa	Justine Clark
Anda	Jasmin Dogar
Achmed	Sarah Martin
Vicar	David Jones
Sir Piggy Wink (The Baron of Boars Hill)	Roy King
His Sons Wink	John Hedge
Nudge	Andrew Black
Flash	Kay Card
Fairy Queen	Jonathan Keen
Sylvia Vetta	Herself
Kenningtonians	Gill Hedge
	Margaret Biggs
	Derek Skipper
Villagers	Jean Rowe
Bogger Joggers	Hazel Wykes
	Margaret Newton
	Sue Sloggett
	Alan Weeks
Spirits of Bagley Wood	Stephanie Johnson
	Tanya Bye
	Tracey Lowe
	Julia Horsley
Children	Susie Black
	Gareth Jones

Script	dialogue	Andrew Black
	lyrics	Shirley Jones
Production		Sylvia Vetta
Musical Director		Jonathan Keen
Pianists		Mrs. Jones
		Jonathan Keen
Choreography		Annette Barrett
Costume		Elizabeth Huxtable
		Pam Skipper
		Jo Purves
		Margaret Biggs
Set & Stage Management		Andrew Black
		Philip Martin
		John Card
		Sue Rolfe
		Bill Rolfe
		Margaret Biggs
Lighting		John Siertsema
Prompt		Shirley Jones
Make Up		Lynn Axe
House Management		Anneke Siertsema

Scene 1 :   Kennington
Scene 2 :   The Road to Bagley Wood

Interval of 20 minutes - refreshments available.

Scene 3 :   In Bagley Wood
Scene 4 :   Kennington

Kennington Players were resurrected as KADS – Kennington Amateur Dramatic Society - in February 1979, following a meeting at the home of Sylvia Vetta. Their first production in 1980 - Son of Ali Baba - The Beggers of Bagley Wood – was performed in January and February 1980, from a script written by Dr Andy Black.

Proceeds from KADS productions continue to benefit other local organisations and charities. This photograph of February 1988 shows Peter Biggs, then chairman of KADS, dressed as Friar Tuck, presenting a cheque for £602 to St Swithun's School head teacher, Mr Michael Allcock, towards school library funds.

May 1980 The nursery unit at St Swithin's School celebrate a donation from Wates Built Homes towards new play equipment. Regional sales manager for Wates, Maurice Edgington, presented the cheque to headteacher, Michael Allcock.

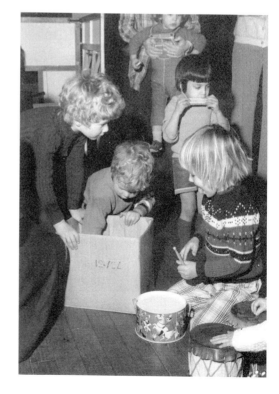

Kennington Toddler Group was started in 1975 by Sylvia Vetta, Mary Dennett, Anneke Siertsema and Elspeth Golding, and was the first of its kind in Oxfordshire. This photograph of 1976 includes the Warner children, Stephen Newton at the back, and Adrian Vetta.

The 21st Kennington Horticultural Show in August 1967 attracted a total of 325 entries. The Kennington Cup for most points in vegetable classes went to Mr H Haytree and the Millenary Cup for flower classes to Mr H Hayter. The Ladies Cup for most points in preserve and cookery classes was won by Mrs F M Hitchen. This photograph shows a class for local children, called 'flowers in an egg cup'.

An early photograph of Kennington Scouts.

The 40th Oxford Kennington Scout Group began in 1940 as a sub-section of the 8th Oxford under the leadership of Mr George Springall of 8th Highfield Scouts. A year later it became the 16th North Berkshire Land Scouts under the leadership of Bill Barnes of 209 Poplar Grove. In 1947 leadership was taken by Thirston Kirk. In 1958 it rejoined the Oxford Association. The group was originally known as Boy Scouts, but renamed Sea Scouts in 1952.

Thurston Kirk, scout leader, with cubs from Cold Arbour, Radley and Kennington on a day trip to Southsea c1944.

In the early days the scout group was led by a Mr Berry and met in the Memorial Hall and the Old Sunday School building, which used to stand on the site of the present-day Health Centre. The headquarters in Otters Reach were purchased in 1942, and these were re-built and reopened as a new hall in 1957. This photograph of May 1957 shows members of Kennington Sea Scouts building these new headquarters – to be called the S S Mayflower – which they hoped to complete for an official opening on Trafalgar Day in October 1957.

Armistice Sunday Parade of Kennington Sea Scouts in 1961, with the Tandem on the right and the old Village Hall on the left.

Kennington Brownie Pack holiday in 1964. Leaders were Eileen Naish and Nina Horwood and the group includes Julie Horwood, Susan Cornell, Linda Hardy, June Rivers, Richard Naish, Jennifer Atkins, Helen Wood, Hilary Ashton, Hilary Perkins and Geoffrey Horwood.

Kennington Guides in 1959 preparing for a hike to the Chiswell Hills. Left to right: Felicity Walkington, Carol -, Denise -, Captain Sylvia Rivers, Tony Rivers, Kathleen -, Kathy Kirby, Mavis Kirby, Fay Mitchell, Sue Monk.

1st Kennington Guides in October 1986.

Members of Kennington Social Club in June 1989, after a marathon 36 hours playing pool to raise money towards the building of the new village youth club. The event was organised by committee member, Nigel Smith.

The Tandem Public House in 1956.

Health Centre

In the 1920s Dr A L B Stevens set up a practice at Green Gables, 326 Abingdon Road, South Oxford, thus becoming the nearest doctor for the residents of Kennington. The first resident doctor was Dr Gerald Shann who moved to 81 Kennington Road in the 1930s and ran a small private practise from a small building in his back garden. After World War II Dr Geoffrey Blackman joined the practise at Abingdon Road as assistant to Dr Stevens, initially lodging with his wife and small baby in rooms upstairs in the Duke of Monmouth public house further along the Abingdon Road.

When Dr Shann retired soon afterwards, Dr Blackman continued to provide medical cover either from Dr Shann's small surgery building, or from the newly built nurses house at 14 The Avenue, or from 'the old larder' of the Barn and Byre on the Kennington Road. He had his own house built at 214 Kennington Road, on the site of four small cottages which had been demolished in 1937.

Dr Blackman's new surgery opened in October 1949, a year after the introduction of the National Health Service. In 1953 Drs Stevens and Blackman took on a new partner, Dr Evan 'Jimmy' James, who moved into Cedar Wood Cottage on The Avenue. In September 1958 Dr Christopher Strode joined the practise, extending his property at 96 Kennington Road to provide surgery accommodation.

Dr Salim Verjee joined the practise in June 1975 and the new Health Centre was opened in June 1976. In 1978 the Health Centre was 'adopted' by the village as the recipient of a special fundraising week, raising £3,000 towards much-needed equipment. Dr Janet Darling joined the practise in 1981, retiring in 2002. Dr James retired in 1983 as did Dr Blackman, with Dr Stuart Frankum taking his place.

Dr Blackman continued to see some patients from his own house and old surgery, but sadly became ill and died in August 1985. His service to the village is commemorated along the footpath leading to the Heath Centre, where there is a large boulder engraved with his name and a small garden planted to his memory.

Dr Strode retired from work in April 1992, being replaced by Dr Rosamond Hall. (Extracted from 'A History of Medical Care in Kennington', courtesy of Kennington History Project and Dr C Strode.)

Dr Darling, Dr Strode, Dr Verjee and Dr Frankcum outside the Kennington Health Centre in 1984.

Sports

Cricket Club 1954. Left to right back row: Mr Coombes, Maurice Petts, Freddie Ball, -, Len Field, Bryn Giles, Peter Peace. Front row: Norman Chasney, Dickie Godfrey, George Butler, Maureen Petts.

Cricket team in the 1960s. Left to right back row: Fred Ball, Fred Trinder, Peter Peace, 'Waddy' Smith, Brian Draper, Les Thompson. Front row: Len Peedell (and son), Bryn Gyles, Len Field, George Butler (and son), Brian Simms.

Kennington Football Team 1953. Left to right back row: Norman Chasney, Frank Walters, Johnny Legge, Peter Peace, Rodger Hamlin, Arthur Berry. Front row: Fred Day, Bryn Giles, Len Peedle, Les Wacknell, George Butler, Len Fields.

Kennington Angling Club in the 1940s. Left to right back row: -, Sid Hughes, -, -, -, -, -. Middle row: Alan Hopgood, Alan Pope, Dick Williamson, Clive Brookes, George Smith, Tom Brookes, -, Reg Hughes. Front row: -, -, Ernie Jones, Ted Dowse, -.

Kennington Angling Club celebration dinner, during the late 1950s. Left to right: Richard Williamson, Tom Brookes, Dr Geoffrey Blackman, George Moss?

Keep Fit team from the Girls Venture Club 1953. Left to right back row: Mary Holcraft, Sally Underwood, Mrs Day instructor, -, Margaret Thomas, Pat -. Front row: Jill Spencer?, Sue Jackson, Glenis Jones, Susan Williamson, Gillian Wyatt, Beryl Reid. This display was being given outside the Village Hall for the Queen's Coronation in 1953.

1951 Kennington Girls Venture Club comic cricket match. Left to right: Margaret Thomas, Audrey Tuffrey(?), Jack Lamper.

The Girls Venture Club was started by Miss Flower, a Brixton school teacher, who started a keep fit class during the war in the village hall. After the war some of the girls took it over and they raised enough money, with the help of a grant, to pay for a keep fit teacher. There was a monthly social when boys were allowed to attend, and in the early 1950s it became a mixed club. The original huts used during the war years were given away to a club at Kingston Bagpuize – they were all dismantled and rebuilt by the boys themselves. The Youth Club was then housed in buildings at the back of the Village Hall, eventually replaced by Jordan Hall, named after Cyril Jordan, the builder who built the Hall at that time.

Kennington Coronation Revels – Saturday 6 June 1953 – Programme of Events. The 'Revels' – mainly sports, had also been held on the river and in the meadows for the Coronation of George VI in 1937.

KENNINGTON CORONATION REVELS

in co-operation with the Coronation Committee

SPORTS PROGRAMME ON KENNINGTON MEADOWS
(Entrance, Tandem Railway Bridge)

SATURDAY, JUNE 6th, commencing 2.30 p.m.

DETAILS OF SPORTS arranged by the MEN'S CLUB
(J. Duffy, Hon. Sec.)

1. MEN'S 100 YARDS SPRINT, over 18 years
2. LADIES' 60 YARDS SPRINT, over 18 years
3. YOUTHS' 80 YARDS SPRINT, 14—18 years
4. GIRLS' 80 YARDS SPRINT, 14—18 years
5. SHOE RACE, Ladies and Gents
6. BUN & TREACLE RACE, Boys and Girls up to 15 years
7. SACK RACE, Gents
8. SACK RACE, Ladies
9. SACK RACE, Boys 14—18 years
10. SACK RACE, Girls 14—18 years
11. MEN'S RELAY (Team of Four), 400 yards Shuttle
12. LADIES' RELAY (Team of Four), 240 yards Shuttle
13. POTATO RACE, Boys and Girls up to 15 years
14. CLOCK RACE, Gents and Ladies
15. THREE-LEGGED RACE, Gents and Ladies
16. THREE-LEGGED RACE, Boys and Girls up to 15 years
17. SLOW CYCLE RACE (own cycle)
18. MEN'S TUG-OF-WAR (teams of eight)

No Entrance Fees. Entries for Races to be made on the Field.
Handicaps to be arranged by the starter in races at his discretion.
Starter: J. C. Smith.   Referee: P. Horton.
Teas and Ices available.   *Sideshows, Competitions, etc.*
Prizes will be presented by Mr. G. A. Hughes at the end of the Sports, approx. 4.30 p.m.
Bring this programme with you, as no other programme will be available on the day.

NOTE *re* PROGRAMME FOR CORONATION DAY
There will be a Fancy Dress Competition for those aged 15 years and upwards.
Assemble Village Hall, 2.30 p.m.   No Entrance Fee

KENNINGTON CRICKET CLUB
present a

A GRAND
Coronation Fete

to be held in
MEMORIAL FIELD, KENNINGTON
SATURDAY, 30th MAY
2.15 p.m.—7.15p.m.
ADMISSION FREE

2.45 p.m. CHILDREN'S SPORTS
5. 0 p.m. CYCLE SPEEDWAY CHALLENGE MATCH
FRED HEBBORN'S FUN-FAIR

Madame Theo, Fortune Teller, Photographer, Pony Rides, Tombola
SIDESHOWS—Darts, Skittles, Aunt Sally, Treasure Hunt, The Diver,
Tossing the Bundle of Hay, Etc.
TEAS, ETC. ON THE GROUND
PRESENTATION OF PRIZES AT 7.15 P.M.

Grand Dance and Talent Competition

in the evening
at Kennington Village Hall
Dancing to the Music of
LAURIE HENDY and his BAND
Spot Prizes   —   ADMISSION 2/6   —   8.30 — 12
Entries for Talent Competition taken on the Evening

All Proceeds from above in aid of Children's Coronation Fund

Kennington Cricket Club also held a Coronation Fete on Saturday 30 May 1953. The programme includes a cycle speedway match between the Kennington Kestrels and Grandpont Giants and a display by the Ixion Motor Cycle Club. Attendees were urged not to forget to visit Madame Theo – 'she will tell you your future' – who was none other than Sylvia Rivers, nee Theobald, with her crystal ball.

It's a Knockout at Forest Side c1974. On the rope are 'Mac' Green at the front, with Alison Rodgers and Sally Woodward behind.

It's a Knockout at Forest Side c1972. Leo Boles is leading the way in this race.

Kennington Boys U10s Team playing at Blackbird Leys c1981. Left to right back row: George Ross manager, Adrian Wappner, Jonathan Dennett, James Warner, Mathew Webb, Alan Purves, Gordon Nixon, Paul Slade, Don White assistant manager. Front row: Kevin Hickman, Neil Downie, Louis Golding, Simon Carpenter, -, -Erskine

Vale of the White Horse Schools Football Trophy 1984. Left to right front row: Richard Allen, Matthew Long, Mark Cox, Allen Jefferies, Paul Evans, James White. Front row: Neil Buckingham, Louis Golding, Bobby Blanco-Rand, David Ross, Richard Fogden, Derek Stirling, Alastair Savanagh. The team were runners up in the final to Dunmore School at Abingdon United's ground at Northcourt Road, Abingdon.

Vale of the White Horse Schools 5-a-side Football 1984. St Swithuns School winners, left to right: Richard Allen, Alaister Cavanah, David Ross, Andy Thomas Oxford United player, Richard Rogden, Matthew Long, Louis Golding.

The formation of Kennington Sports Club

The following is a report from original records regarding the proposed 'new' recreation ground to be built at Playfield Road.

'Kennington Sports Club held a large Fete and Sports Day on Saturday 25 June 1955 at the sports ground in Bagley Wood Road, with an evening dance at Kennington Village Hall. The sports programme catered for all ages, and was well supported by local businesses and advertising. The Village has acquired a piece of land some five acres in extent, situated between the Memorial Field on the south and the Well at Little London on the north side. This piece of land, while being no Kennington Oval, is capable of being transformed into a desirable playing field. Work is shortly to be started by Messrs Sutton & Sons of Reading to achieve this. In April of this year, the Parish Council convened a public meeting as a result of which the Kennington Sports Club has been formed, to add yet another to the many thriving organisations in the Village. A Pavilion has been purchased, and is due to be erected on the field in the near future. Cricket, Football and Tennis Sections of the Sports Club are organised all with representatives on the Committee, ready for the 1954 season, when we hope the Sports Ground will be ready'.

Work started on the field on Monday 12 October 1953.

Businesses and Shops

176 Kennington Road – newsagents, seen here in 1955, before the building of the side extension. This was built in the early 1930s by Mr and Mrs John Barson, who lived above the shop with their family, Charles, Arthur, Ada and May. Arthur ran the business after the death of his parents, with help from his sister, Ada.

Arthur had been badly injured in World War I and never fully recovered, and suffered a stroke at the age of 57. Ada, born in 1907, never married and remained at home, at 6 Kenville Road, to look after her brother. Their sister, May Barson married Mr Acaster and lived at 9 Kenville Road. The business was sold to Mr and Mrs W J Kear.

In 1954 the business was purchased by Mr and Mrs Stanley Shires. Upon retirement in 1965 they sold to the Maynard family, who, in turn, sold it to the Dillons group of newsagents. The business closed in 2002 and is now being converted to a private house.

Mr and Mrs Stanley Shires in the garden of 176 Kennington Road in 1960. Next to the newsagents is an alley leading to Upper Road. At this time, the butchers shop, next door to the alley, was run by Mr and Mrs Milton and their son Brian.

Les Belcher and his property at 172 Kennington Road in the 1980s.

This block of houses date back to the 1880s, being some of the original houses in the village. This was the residence of Leslie Belcher who moved into the house in 1922, until his death in 1988, when the property was sold and became Smiths the Chemists. Les joined the army as a drummer boy at the beginning of World War I, when he was only 15, and served in the Oxford and Bucks Light Infantry, before moving to the regiment of the Black Watch, of which he was very proud. Les was well known in the village and enjoyed visiting the Tandem public house and the company of many friends. A keen gardener, he made the gardens of number 172 very much admired. He worked at Osberton Radiators, in north Oxford, and would cycle there and back daily. His family consisted of one daughter and two granddaughters.

No 174 Kennington Road was occupied in 1939 by George Moody, later by a Mrs Acock and then by Mr and Mrs Brown. It was turned into a butcher shop by Mr Milton, who then sold it to the co-op. It was bought by Mr Clive Calver, also as a butchers, from 1969 to 1992. In the early years Mr Calver bought an old Elliston & Cavell removal van and converted it into a travelling butcher shop, fully equipped with refrigeration.

On the opposite side of the road, next to The Tandem public house, was 181 Kennington Road, Sybils Wool Shop, selling babies clothes and knitting wools, run by a Miss S Corbey in 1960. Next door, 179 Kennington Road, was earlier the Cadena Cake Shop, later Sid Gordon Cakes, and then another grocery shop run, in the 1960s, by a Mr and Mrs C Haydon and known as Lesbies.

Clive Calver with daughter Tracy, in the butchers at 174 Kennington Road, July 1992.

The building on the left, 168 Kennington Road, now the co-operative, was a general grocery store run, from about 1938, by Mr William Wiggins, at which time it also served as the post office.

No 166 Kennington Road, now Kennington Flooring Company, occupies the premises of a former hardware shop owned by Peter Finch. No 162 Kennington Road was occupied, in 1939, by B V Finch plumber.

This shop in The Avenue was built by Mr Mills in 1952, who also built the Kennington garage next door. It was occupied by Robert Purvey for approximately seven years. Mr Purvey had moved from Hinksey into the newly built 27 Poplar Grove in 1938. The shop at first sold cycles, then later ironmongery. The property was absorbed into the garage building, becoming part of the showroom facing the main Kennington Road. To the left of Purveys was a tiny chemists shop, *'crammed with all sorts of things and smelling of rubber water bottles. They sold all sorts of things, cameras, thermos flasks, batteries.'* It was originally Vales the Chemist and then kept by Mr and Mrs Ault, but closed due to competition from the ironmongers and the post office nearby.

Bottom right: Purveys shop, showing the building of the garage to the right in 1953.

R H Purvey, 21B The Avenue, cycle agent, in 1953.

Mr and Mrs Alfred Carpenter started a grocery shop at 183 Poplar Grove, later owned and run by Mr Jack Ridgeway. '*This was a general grocery store, sold practically everything. They used to have the biscuit tins around in front of the counter. We used to cut across from school, down through the fields.*' The property is now a private bungalow opposite Manor Grove.

Two shops were built at the junction of Poplar Grove and Meadow View in the early 1960s. Originally a butchers shop on the right, whose last owner was Mr David Avery, and a co-operative store on the left. Jim and Lynne Hardiman bought the grocery business from Mr and Mrs Trinder on 13 August 1983. There was another butchers shop, owned by Harry Revell from before the Second World War, situated on Red Bridge, opposite Touchwood Sports. Mr Palmer later ran it as a butchers shop for a while, but this little building is now derelict, last used as Spokes Cycles.

Mr Alfred Alfonso Rogers started a coat-hanger factory from 135 Upper Road. This property was demolished to make way for Rowles Close. '*Mr Rogers owned all that land right from the front to the back of the paper shop before Rowles Close was built. He operated from a little hut with a little stone cottage in front of it and they used to make coat-hangers. He expanded and moved to Sandford Lane in the early 1950s, into an old nissan hut, where he employed about a dozen people. It's an industrial estate now. Before that he used to send work to 'out-workers' and my aunty used to do them in her shed up at Sugworth Lane.*' About 1954 the business was taken over by Wardray & Co, light metal workers.'

Extract from Oxford Times 18 January 1952:

Kennington Engineer's Claim
By using a new technique, a Kennington engineer claims that houses for the 4,200 people on Oxford's housing list could be built in about six months. He is Mr Alfred A Rogers of 135 Upper Road, Kennington, a coat-hanger manufacturer, who says he has devised a method, which, by using pre-cast concrete units, would cut building costs by half. Mr Rogers has patented the idea and given plans and particulars to Mr Lawrence Turner, MP, who has handed them on to the Minister of Housing and Local Government, Mr Harold Macmillan. Mr Rogers who lives in a bungalow behind which a small number of employees are making coat-hangers, has had many set-backs with his plan for marketing the scheme. Last June, a fire destroyed his workshop at Radley, causing several thousand pounds damage. Later his premises were burgled and equipment stolen. He also hopes to market a pedestrian crossing, and particulars about this have been sent to the Ministry of Transport. For about £25 Mr Rogers says he can erect either temporary or permanent crossings. These comprise small rails on each side of the road and a system of lights set into operation by pedestrians walking over a depression mat.

The Ministry of Transport was obviously interested in the potential of this new type of pedestrian crossing, the brain-child of Mr Alfred Rogers and Mr J Walker of Radley, as reported in the Oxford Times of 14 March 1952. At that time council officials visited 135 Upper Road to inspect a model of this new crossing which had been erected on a path at the rear of Mr Roger's home. It is not known whether this prototype was ever adapted for use.

The Post Office at 156 Kennington Road. This building is on the corner of Edward Road, which was previously known as Lewis Road, reputedly after the name of an early postmaster. The road was renamed in 1936 after King Edward VIII, who subsequently abdicated the throne. The post office was run for many years by Mr and Mrs Geoffrey Faulkner, and was purchased in 1962 by Derek and Joy Ledger.

Extensions were started a few years later, and the new building was put up around the existing building. A side extension was opened as 'Joanne' a wool and baby linen shop, run by Joy Ledger. The premises were sold to Mr Hancock, whose wife ran the baby linen shop for fifteen years. Alan Donahue then took over and he removed the name 'Joanne' from the premises. The premises are now operated as a veterinary surgeons with a separate post office next door.

No 80 Kennington Road, on the corner of Kenville Road is another grocery shop (later the VG and now the Spar Shop). It had originally been a dairy built by Pyes in 1930 for Mr and Mrs Jack Gibbons *'who delivered milk around the village in his pony and trap, and later on his motorbike and sidecar, and taught my son to swear!'* During 1939 it was known as Kennington Dairy, with part of it serving as a hairdressers known as Eyles & Pledge, later run by Grace Enoch. Bill Ledger extended the property and turned it into a self service store – the Corner Stores.

Dave and Ron Crawford, father and son, previous owners of the VG stores, who bought the premises from Arthur Young, owner until the early 1980s.

At 80 Kennington Road, the Corner Stores - now known as Kennington Stores - was sold to Mike and Jane Clarke in October 1983. The above photograph shows the original shop face at this time, note the original dairy corner door and the window blinds. The shop was extended to the side, almost doubling the shop space. The Clarkes remained in the village until December 1996. During the 1980s the VG operated as The Late Shop, open seven days a week from 7.00 a.m. until 10.00 p.m.

At 74 Kennington Road, believed to have been known as Merwede in the 1930s, there was an unusual property, originally a wooden lean-to shed, run by Charlie Cosendey - a Swiss gent. He is obviously well remembered in the village:

'He stocked everything you could want. This was originally a large tin shed and it was called Kennington Tea Gardens. He later had this village shop built with flats over it. Charlie had a speech impediment and was very difficult to understand, but he made delicious ice-cream, ha'penny cornets sold everyday, including Sundays.'

'To visit his shop you didn't go into the shop, you used to open a flap on the front and drop it down. That was his counter and you stood outside to get served.'

'During hot spells of weather, and rations being available, he used to sell 'home made' ice cream. My brother and his friends used to be employed to turn the handle of the churn – payment being in the form of a free wafer or two!'
In 1960 Mr R A Williamson, grocer, occupied the premises.

34-36 Kennington Road were farm buildings before the Second World War, owned and used by Horace Walker, poultry farmer, and his wife, Edith. Mr Walker owned a considerable amount of land in this part of Kennington, including the gravel pits and up to the end of Kennington Lane and extending in the other direction as far as the Stone House. During the war these premises were used industrially by Mr Rodger, making coat hangers for American servicemen. Mr Walker's daughter, Doreen, married Bill Smith and they started a plastic injection moulding business, named Heathrod Ardwyn, from numbers 34-36 Kennington Road. The business was successful and employed some 40 people, mostly local people. The business expanded and moved to Radley in the late 1960s. The Kennington Road premises were let to an engineering company, and then taken over by BSK Motors, occupying part of the original farm buildings. The other buildings were rebuilt in 1982 and are now occupied by Hamonox motor repairs.

The fire at 34-36 Kennington Road in 1982, which destroyed some of the original farm buildings.

SECTION SIX

Demolition and Development

The main development of Kennington occurred in 1913, when the Estate of approximately 282 acres, was broken up and sold by Edgar Norton Disney by auction. This auction was held in a tent on Lot 12 on Tuesday 13 May 1913.

The Estate was described as '*comprising practically the whole of the Picturesque Village of Kennington, which is admirably situated, being sheltered by Woodland and approached from Abingdon through a fine Avenue of Trees, which form part of the Kennington Manor Farm. Splendid Views of Oxford and the surrounding Country, including one of the prettiest Reaches of the River Thames, may be obtained from many parts of the Estate.*'

The sale catalogue continues '*The Building Sites are particularly attractive. The demand for Cottages and Bungalows in the neighbourhood of Oxford is far in excess of the supply, and the Sites on this Estate offer every facility for the profitable erection of this class of Property, being near to the City and within a few minutes walk of the Halt Station.*' The map attached to the sale catalogue indicated the layout of New Roads 'abutting on Lots 1, 2 and 3' and provided for the future development of these roads by the Local Authority.

The following sale prices have been annotated in a copy of the 1913 sale catalogue belonging to Frank Luckett of The Chalet, Kennington, who was, we could deduce, present at the actual auction.

Lots 1 to 14 were all building plots of various sizes. Lot 1 no offer: Lot 2 £50: Lot 3 £30: Lot 4 £30: Lot 5 £30: Lot 6 no bid: Lot 7 no bid: Lot 8 to 13 are not annotated: Lot 14 £30: Lot 15 – Manor Farm and four cottages - £5,300: Lot 16 withdrawn: Lot 17 withdrawn: Lot 18 £50: Lot 19 (the buildings now converted into Social Club) £230: Lot 20 £95: Lot 21 cottages occupied by Mr R Gibbons at rent of £2 12sh, Mrs Greenaway at rent of £5 4sh and Mrs Steptoe at rent of £5 4sh reached £145: Lot 22 three cottages, one vacant the others held by Mrs Mundy of Manor Farm fetched £160: Lot 23 – two cottages occupied by Mr G Gibbins and Mr J Villabois at rent of £7 16sh each was sold for £175: Lot 24 was a cottage held by Mr Allen and sold for £260; Lot 25 cottage held by Mr F East at rental of £12 per annum fetched £160: Lots 26, 27 and 28 building sites were withdrawn: Lot 29 a small building site in Little London Lane held by Miss Slay at a rental of £1 per annum was sold for £16: Lot 30 6 acres of meadow land known as Fiddlers Elbow sold for £105. Lots 31 to 38 were sold as freehold ground rents with existing houses already let on 999 year leases.

It is interesting to note that a Mrs M Luckett was living at 45 Upper Road in 1939: was this the plot purchased by Frank Luckett, the owner of this particular sale catalogue?

This original village hall, known as The Memorial Hall, stood adjacent to 165 Kennington Road, directly opposite the bottom of Edward Road.

The 'new' Village Hall was opened on 6 June 1940, having been converted from a barn originally belonging to the Manor Estate, with an adjacent cow shed, on the left, being converted into social club rooms. The Village Hall was demolished in April 1987, and, at the same time, the children's recreation ground in front of the social club was redeveloped.

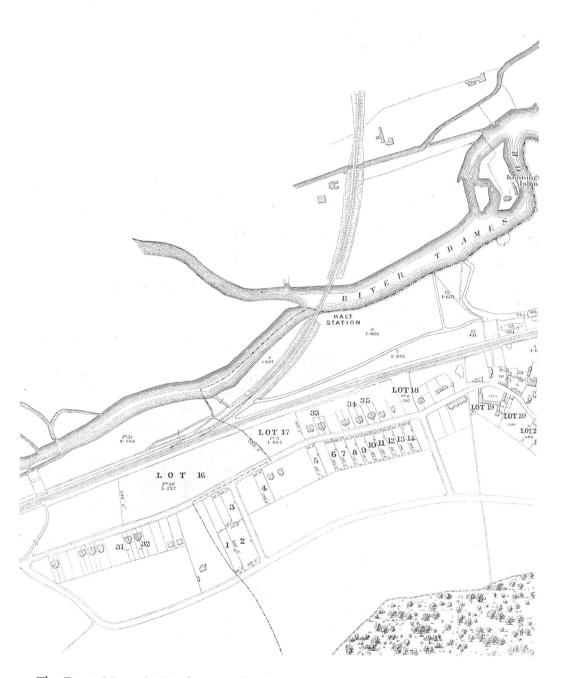

The Estate Map of 1913 showing the division into Lots for purchase at auction.

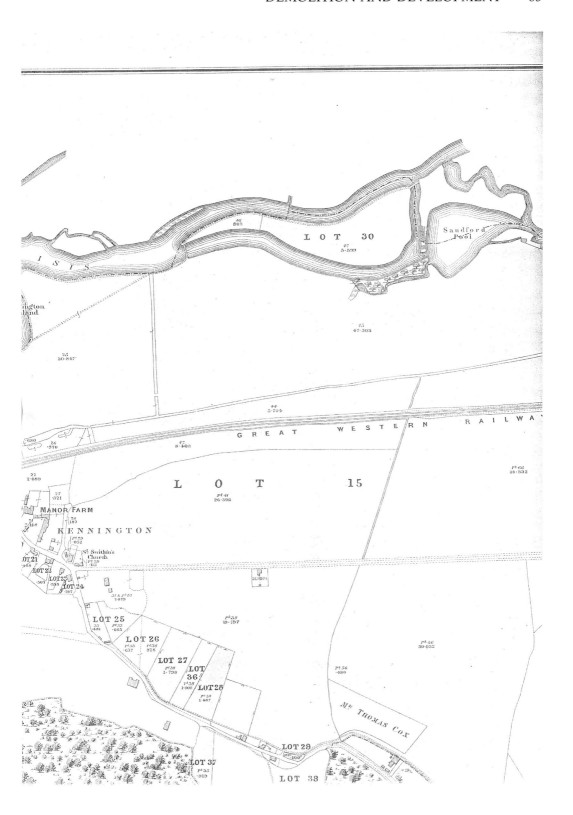

Kennington villagers cutting the first sod on the site of the new village centre in 1987. Left to right: George Ross clerk to the parish council, Ted Perkins, Rob Maggs, Dennis Robins, -, -, Phil Stevens, Roger Dennett chair of the parish council, Valerie Holland, Mike Holland, David Goldsworthy, Derek Skipper, Doris Francis, Margaret Biggs, 'Johnnie' Kirby, Hettie Perkins, Rose Taylor, Jean Lloyd, Joan Bowen-Thomas. Children in front are the Skipper twins with Sarah Biggs in the centre.

Roger Dennett, chairman of both the parish council and the centre's project committee, was given the honour of the ceremonial spadework, but only after a JCB had been brought in to dig up the tarmac where the old village hall used to stand.

Another view of this event, showing the wartime wooden buildings that were used as the youth club. This, too, was eventually demolished. New youth club premises were opened in 1989 by Mrs Doreen Kirby, affectionately known to all as 'Johnnie', who served as one of its youth leaders for almost thirty years.

The Village Centre was opened in December 1988. It consisted of a large 200 seat hall with a sprung maple floor, a new county library, three conference rooms, stage and modern facilities. The project had taken some four years to come to fruition, at a cost of almost £350,000, with Kennington villagers raising some £12,000 towards this cost.

Roger Dennett, George Ross and John Jones at the unveiling of the plaque commemorating the opening of the new hall. The plaque was unveiled by Mr John Jones, leader of Vale of the White Horse Council, which provided grants for half the cost.

Templeton College donated a 20-foot ten-year old red oak from its grounds as a gift to the village, which was planted adjacent to the new Village Hall.

Mrs C Lancelot Harman, wife of the managing director of Hunt Edmunds Brewery, unveiled the Scholar Gipsy inn sign on 7 June 1957.

The Scholar Gipsy public house on Kennington Road was named in honour of Matthew Arnold's famous poem *The Scholar Gipsy*. Demolotion commenced on 13 June 2001. The land was developed by Berkeley Homes Limited as the Bookman Court Development, but was renamed Ross Court in 2002, commemorating the retirement of parish clerk, George Ross, after 25 year service.

Kennington Garage Service Station from the main Kennington Road

Kennington Garage Service Station was built c1953 and closed for business in 2002. *'Mr Mills built the garage and he worked on it at the weekends. After the garage he had a very large cabin cruiser along the side of Poplar Grove on the left where all the cars are now. He spent about 2 or 3 years renovating this cruiser and then he took it on the Thames and sailed up and down. Then he sold the garage and went to Australia.'*

Bridie Murphy worked at the garage for almost 30 years, until its closure in 2002. In 1965 the proprietor, Mr Ray Barlow, took over the franchise of the Simca car and the business expanded. In 1969 he had converted the adjacent buildings, one time chemist shop and store, as part of extended showrooms. At the time of closing the business belonged to Mrs Ann Barlow. The site will be developed for housing.

The old pavilion buildings on Forest Side playing fields, summer 1999, during the Bagley Wood Fun Run. At this time materials were already being stacked on the field, ready for the new building.

The new pavilion was built adjacent to the old buildings and was opened on 15 May 2000. A plaque was unveiled by John Rowe, chairman of Kennington Playing Fields Association.

The opening of the new pavilion. Left to right: Terry Fletcher, Colin Charlett, Phil Stevens, -Bowler, Bob Johnson, Gerry Patterson at back, Pam Johnson, -, Alex Glass, Jackie Forster, Carole Ross, Doreen Horseman, -, -, Mark Horseman, Ian Sillince, George Ross, John Rowe.

Patsie Tait standing in fields, looking towards Cowley. This area is now the middle stretch of Poplar Grove, formerly known as Poplar Road. The top end of Poplar Grove was built first, together with the bungalows at the bottom end. For many years the middle section was open fields. The road commemorates the large number of Poplar trees which used to grow at the northern end of the road.

The Cold Store, which was demolished in the 1980s to allow for housing development, now Otters Reach. The Cold Store was opened in July 1942 by the Ministry of Food, for the storage and distribution of frozen carcasses to army and airforce bases.

Nos 64 to 68 Kennington Road in July 1956. The field behind was part of the old golf links and later developed for Simpsons Way and other roads.

Houses in Upper Road in July 1956, taken from near the top of Edward Road. The road on the left is Bagley Close.

This early photograph shows the cottages which used to stand on what is now the Tandem car park.

No 50 Kennington Road – The Lawsons – in 1965

This property was built in 1914, on a double plot purchased by Walter Doman, woodsman, and brother to Harold Doman. From approximately 1939 to 1947 it was occupied by Mr and Mrs Alfred Merry as tenants, before the Doman family moved back in. This photograph clearly shows the concrete block structure, blocks manufactured in the village. One or two other present-day properties still retain this original block finish.

No 52 Kennington Road – The Retreat – was built for a butler from Radley College, at the back of the same plot.

No 54 Kennington Road – The Bungalow

This property, again on a double plot, was built in 1902 by Mr Jarvis, who had premises in St Aldates, Oxford. For many years it was occupied by Mr and Mrs Gifford-Ambler who used it as a summer retreat, spending their winters at Somerton in Somerset. It was left empty for several years during the early 1960s and became somewhat derelict, before being sold in 1966. The present owners have carefully modernised the building, whilst retaining its original exterior.

No 56 Kennington Road – The Nook – is another original property in Kennington, probably built around the same time. It was occupied by the Savage family in 1925, later by the Rev. Edwin James.

The Lawns, now situated in Jackson Drive, was originally the next property along Kennington Road. Laid back from the main road, it had an extensive frontage and drive – *'with peacocks on the front lawn'*. This property was built in 1908, also by Mr Jarvis.

Festival, Celebration and Events

1953 Coronation Party in Poplar Grove. Children left to right: -, Linda Hamlet, David Hartigan, -Saunders. Adults: Cyril Villebois, Mrs Caddock with baby, Mrs Workman, Mrs Grant in distance.

1953 Coronation Party in Poplar Grove. Graham Pitts, Bob Purvey, Ken Shaw, Pat Woodley.

Kennington Overseas Aid held many events to raise funds, culminating annually in the week long Kennington Festival. This photograph taken during the 1970s is of participants in a stretcher race, stopping for refreshment outside the VG Store at the corner of Kenville Road. Left to right: Terry Fifield, -Fifield, Kevin Dighton.

Cheerleaders at Kennington Festival in 1979

The proceeds of Kennington Festival Week in June 1979 went towards equipment for Kennington Health Centre. The Festival Princess was Mandy Jones, with Julie Hardy and Lisa Clark as her attendants, chosen by Dr and Mrs Geoffrey Blackman and Brian Hartigan, who had been voted Football Player of the Year.

Kennington Festival June 1981 and the winning float entered by the mums and dads of Kennington Playgroup, portraying Captain Pugwash and his pirate crew. Runners up were the local Brownies imitating the Muppets and third place went to Bob and Mary Bakewell's 'Star Truck'.

Kennington Methodist church entered a World of Sport float in the Kennington festival in June 1981.

A Festival float prepared by the Brownies and Guides c1971.

1983 Kennington Festival, and a group of Brownies at Templeton College.

1986 Festival float from the Brownies was on the lines of 'Mary, Mary quite contrary'.

1977 Silver Jubilee celebrations at Bagley Close

Two residents, George Ross and Margaret White, organised this event, involving all the residents of the Close. Initially they contacted every household and extracted promises of food. On the day George Ross recalls how apprehensive they were. '*All the tables had been set out, and I was worried that no-one would turn up. Then someone walked out and plonked a plate of doughnuts in the middle – suddenly everyone was coming out of their houses and the tables were covered with plates of food. It was a tremendous success.*'

Children's Party – 1977 Silver Jubilee Celebrations

Hettie and Frank Perkins with grandchildren are in the middle of this group of residents.

Various contests were organised, including the Drag Queen competition above. The winner was Don White.

The Ladies Jubilee Hat competition. Mrs Breeze is in the centre with the tall hat, Janet Morris on left in white dress. Other competitions included Fancy Dress and Best Table Decoration.

More than forty local children performed The Christmas Jazz, a Nativity play at Kennington Methodist church in 1983.

An RAC Pioneer Rally in 1949 attracted large crowds when the vintage cars passed through Kennington.

Watched by the Rev. Rodney Cox, Mrs Hilda Robinson, of Bayworth Manor, lays the foundation stone of the new Methodist Church at Kennington in March 1967. Two hundred people attended the ceremony, conducted by Kennington's minister, the Rev. Rodney Cocks, and the benediction was given by the Rev. Donald Rose, Superintendent of the Oxford Methodist Circuit. Up to this date Kennington Methodists had worshipped in their own homes, or hired the village hall for services.

Right: Miss Edith Gandy in 1967

Miss Gandy lived at 192 Upper Road, a property occupied in 1925 by Edward Gandy, and known as 'Green Close'. Miss Gandy was a staunch Methodist, and sold the land adjoining her property for the new Methodist church. She had started the first Kennington guide pack and had a guide hut built on a piece of land next to her house.

Methodist church choir c1973. Left to right: Rev Neil Richardson and wife Rhiannon, Geoff Thompson, David Cowlett, Tom and Marjorie Gibson, Lynn Johnson, Peter Cowlett, Maisie Johnson, Trevor Cowlett, Joan Cobb, Brenda Cowlett.

Members of the Young Wives Club organised many activities to organise funds for the new St Swithuns Church building in 1956. Left is Audrey Hartigan with Mrs Ainsley on the right.

The Beating of the Parish Bounds in 1986.

In March 1986, over 100 parishioners took part in a repeat of the Beating of the Bounds ceremony of 1936, which involved walking round three miles of the parish boundaries, starting at Templeton College, through Bagley Wood and the village itself to Sandford. All ages took part, including a handful of people who had been at the original ceremony fifty years previously.

The group in Bagley Wood.

Half way round the walk, in the garden of the Isis public house. The Isis is within Kennington parish boundary. Left to right: Sylvia Boyes, Margaret Simpson, Jean Dearson, -, Kath Suckling. Front row: Vaughn Haskins, Peggy Cox.

A Thanksgiving service was held on 16 March 1986 at St Swithuns Church. Extract of an address given at that time by Roger Dennett, chairman of Kennington Parish Council: *'It is indeed my privilege to make this address on this occasion of thanksgiving – giving thanks to God for fifty years of Kennington as a civil parish. It is even more pleasurable because we have George Simpson here with us and he is the only surviving member of the 1936 Parish Council. In fact his name will live on long after this service tonight because the Chair of Office of the Chairman of Kennington Parish Council – and I am wearing it tonight – was presented to the Council by George. Kennington can be described as a 'young community with very ancient roots'. Kennington is known to have existed as perhaps a small hamlet in the fifth century A.D. The Oxford Dictionary of Placenames states that the earliest record is 821, when it was called CHENITUN – the tun of Cenas' people. A tun was an enclosure/fence round a homestead, which eventually became a village. In 956 King Edwin granted a charter giving CENIGTON to Brightholm, his favourite priest who had been residing in the Abbey of Abingdon. Over the years our village has had many names, all derived from CHENITUN, up until today when we are Kennington.*

In 1803 the township of Kennington was enclosed by an Act of Parliament and in 1809 Sir George Bowyer of Radley bought the entire estate. Sir George built the Avenue in order to provide a better and more direct access from Oxford to Radley! In 1844 the Great Western Railway reached Oxford – the population of Kennington was about 150 at this time.

On 13 May 1913, the birthday of modern Kennington, the Estate was divided into 38 lots to be auctioned in order to pay off the debts associated with Sir George Bowyer's ambitious schemes. In 1936 Kennington became a civil parish and the first parish council was formed. 1956 saw the celebration of 1000 years of the village of Kennington – 1000 years from when King Edwin granted the charter.

Now, in 1986 we celebrate the fact that the civil parish of Kennington was formed on 16 March 1936 – 50 years ago to the actual date.'

After the service tea and refreshments were served, which included a cake baked by local councillor, Frances Hitchen. Left to right: George Ross clerk to the parish council in 1986, Roger Dennett chair in 1986, with George Simpson, aged 90, first clerk to the parish council in 1936.

Kennington Boundaries

Kennington has natural boundaries: to the west lies Bagley Wood, to the east the water meadows and the river. These boundaries, together with the railway line have determined the shape and development of Kennington, which extended north and south between these constraints.

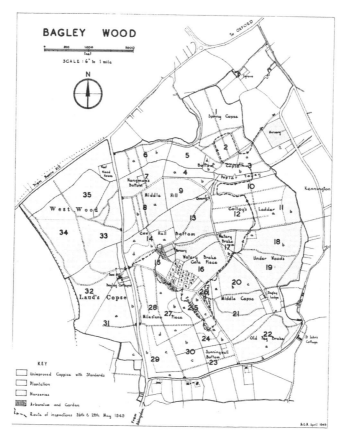

Bagley Wood

Map of Bagley Wood in 1949, prepared by St John Baptist College, Oxford, and contained in the booklet 'Retrospect and Prospect 1949'. Note the Nursery in the top right hand corner, now the site of Forest Side Recreation Ground, from which the new development of Old Nursery View derives its name. The road name, Colley Wood, was named after Colley's Ladder plantation, seen on the middle right. To the left can be seen West Wood House, and Bagley Saw Mill and Cottages. In 1949 the area of Bagley Wood was 566 acres, comprising 163 acres under plantation, 315 acres under coppice, chiefly with oak, and 88 acres of roads, paths, ditches, the sites of the three cottages and the sawmill, and three small paddocks.

The Wood formed part of a royal estate until it was granted to the Abbey of Abingdon in the second half of the tenth century. The Crown took possession in 1538 following the dissolution of the abbey. On 18 December 1552 *'the woodland called Baggle Common'* was granted to Henry Herdson who, on 25 March 1553, sold the Wood for £160 to Sir John Mason, knight, an Abingdon man. On 31 October 1557 Mason sold to St John's College for £270 that portion of the Wood *'which is and lies next towards the city of Oxford, that is to say from the way or bound there newly made through the wood from Kennington field near unto Colly Launder stile on the east part unto the Queen's highway leading from Abingdon to Oxford on the west part'*. The other portion of the Wood was sold to St John's College for £300 on 10 February 1584. The College therefore had possession of the whole of the Wood east of the Oxford-Abingdon road. The portion of the west of this road was controlled by the manors of Sunningwell and Bayworth, and was also seized by the Crown in 1538. In 1610 St John's College started negotiations to purchase *'all that parcel of waste, woodground, common and coppice ground, commonly called Westwood and West Baglye alias Bagly Common in Bagly, lying in Radley and situate between the highway leading from Oxford to Abingdon on the east'*. The sale was not completed until 6 July 1619 for the sum of £600.

The Bagley Wood staff in 1949. Left to right back row: William Cross, Les Hewer, S Hulme, Jimmy Godfrey, John Doman. Middle row: Bill Gray (Wood Manager and also Manager of the Research Nursery at Kennington), R Hart-Synnot (Bursar of St John's College), Harry Doman (Head Woodman, and nephew of Michael Doman). Front row: P Guntrip and Freddie Godfrey (no relation to Jimmy Godfrey). The staff comprised a wood manager, a head woodman, a sawyer, a tractor-driver, two foresters and an apprentice, plus two pensioners for occasional work. The weekly wagebill in 1949 was about £38.

Bagley Cottage was built in 1868, with a large room attached to it for the *'purpose of College entertainments'*. This entertainment included shooting rights within Bagley Wood.

The River and Rose Island

Looking across the water meadows behind the Tandem, during the 1930s. These, and the river, were natural boundaries for Kennington village.

On the right of the photograph is the paddock where Horace Chasney, one-time landlord of The Tandem, used to keep poultry. *'The meadow behind the Tandem, we used to call that Snipe's Meadow because the snipes used to be down there. And it was full of snakes heads — you don't see them now.'* The cottages on the left used to be occupied at that time by the Villebois, Daniels and Smith families. These were pulled down after 1947.

Memories of Rose Island by Mrs Dolly Trueman, whose mother used to run The Swan public house on Kennington Island.

'It was a small island in the Thames opposite the village of Kennington, about two and a half miles from Oxford, in between Iffley and Sandford Locks. Sometimes it is called Kennington Island, sometimes Swan Island or Rose Island. Rose Island is its original name.

We used to walk from Iffley towards a landing stage opposite the island from which a punt ferried customers back and forth to the pub on the island. Sometimes there were as many as twenty people in the punt, and it was a case of keeping sober otherwise we might have fallen in the river. The pub was called The Swan, and it closed about 1928. It was a favourite with college boat crews who often used to stop off there for a few refreshing pints. It was kept by Bill Whitfield and his wife, Caroline, just after the First World War. Her brother, George Gills, from Cranham Street in Jericho, worked for a short time on the ferry punt, helping out the regular man from Littlemore.'

Rose Island in Edwardian times

Rose Island, and the Swan public house, which was sold into private hands in 1928.

Apparently the island was purchased in 1633 by Crooke and Hugh Barker's Charity, which was connected with the Oxford City Church of St Michael at the North Gate. The income was used to support the church, which explains why the island is sometimes known by yet another name: St Michael's Isle.

Morlands Brewery bought the island in 1883 at which time there was already a pub there, and six years later sold it to Morrells. In 1919 its lease was assigned to a firm called Country Hostels who ran a small and highly exclusive hotel.

A London barrister, Mr George Hesketh, and his wife Sonia lived there from 1954, at which time the pub lounge was the drawing room, and outside, what used to be the skittle alley, served as a games room for the Hesketh children.

Rose Island viewed from the towpath.

This stretch of river has been known to freeze over, as seen in this photograph taken 11 February 1895. On occasions there was a sheep roast on the ice in front of the pub. This event was evidently recorded on a large carved mantel inside the pub - but this has long since disappeared.

The Railway

The Great Western Railway Company was formed in 1833, with the aim of constructing a railway line between London and Bristol. Great Western appointed Isambard Kingdom Brunel to build its railway. However, it was not until June 1844 that the branch line from Didcot to Grandpont Station in Oxford was opened. This line bi-sected the Manor Farm land at Kennington. On 2 September 1850 the Oxford and Rugby Railway Company opened a line from Oxford to Banbury, extended in 1852 to Birmingham.

At this time Kennington was still a small village passed by trains travelling between London and Oxford. The railway at this point was in low-lying land, some 15 inches or so lower than it is today, and very close to the River Thames. During winter months flooding was very common and caused consideration disruption to the railway. At these times horses were used to draw the carriages through the water, as described in 1852. *'The trains to London were stopped at Kennington Crossing between two and three miles south of the Oxford station and about quarter of a mile south of the water. The engine was shifted to the rear of the carriages, which it pushed to the water's edge; horses were then harnessed to them, and the carriages drawn by them through the water. At the other side the engine which was to take the train on to Oxford was waiting; this engine was accompanied by a pilotman who received his instructions from an Inspector of Police (railway), who was stationer on the South side of the water. The actual time required to pass a train through the water was about 12 minutes.'* Eventually the line was raised and, with additional drainage work, the problem of regular flooding was solved.

In October 1864 Kennington became a junction with the opening by the Wycome Railway Company of its broad-gauge branch from Thame. At Kennington the railway crossed the River Thames via a 270ft wooden viaduct. In 1902 a new signal box was constructed on the Kennington side of the branch line and replaced an earlier box that used to stand on the Oxford side, installed during the 1870s. The new signal box at Kennington Junction was built of brick with a slate roof containing a 43-lever frame.

In February 1908 a new steam railmotor service was introduced between Oxford and Princes Risborough, resulting in two new halts (miniature stations) at Kennington. The first was at Abingdon Road Halt, built on the village side of the Red Bridge, at a cost of £474, the second one was called Iffley Halt, although lying much closer to Kennington than to Iffley and this cost £201. This service was not a success and was withdrawn in 1915 and the halts were dismantled.

In July 1942 a Ministry of Food cold store was opened at Kennington, on the site of Otters Reach. This was provided with its own rail siding, which was removed on 28 June 1969, with the cold store itself being demolished during the 1980s. During the war the railway at Kennington was very busy, and the running of goods trains was often disrupted by air raids in the London area, preventing the onward travel of these trains.

(With acknowledgement to the Kennington History Project publication – The Railway at Kennington).

Kennington Junction Signal Box in 1960 with 'St Peters Hall' train in front

Kennington Junction, together with all manual signal boxes in the area, was closed in 1973 following the opening of the electric power signal box at Oxford station.

Kennington Viaduct - this photograph was taken by Mr Doman on 11 November 1923

In 1923 the railway bridge over the Thames was replaced by a new girder bridge, and the old bridge removed. There was originally a wooden viaduct here, which had been replaced by a steel girder bridge in about 1880.

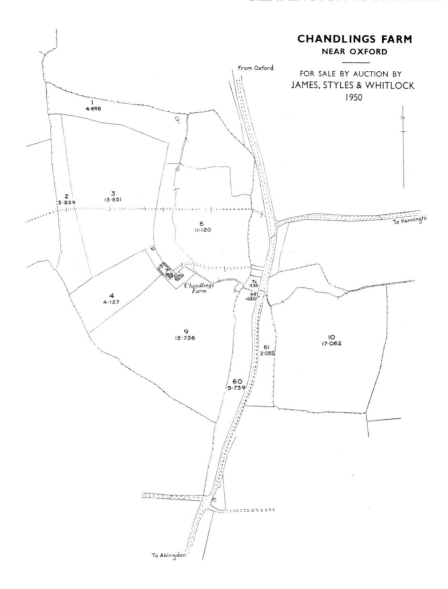

CHANDLINGS FARM
NEAR OXFORD

FOR SALE BY AUCTION BY
JAMES, STYLES & WHITLOCK
1950

Chandlings Farm

Location map of Chandlings Farm, when put up for sale by Christ Church college, by auction, in 1950. The details stated '*Chandlings Farmhouse is a very interesting old house, dating probably from the Seventeenth Century, mainly stone built and tiled with partly slated roof. Its situation is truly delightful, being on high ground approached from the Abingdon Road by a most pleasant drive and completely secluded. The accommodation comprises a Small Hall, two Sittingrooms of fair dimensions, a Large Kitchen fitted with Raeburn stove, Bathroom with fitted bath and wash basin, 3 Good Bedrooms and a Boxroom or Small Bedroom, front and back staircases.*' The farm buildings at that time included a stone and slated range of cow sheds with modern cement floor and mangers for 8 head, cemented yard, range of three modern brick and slated pig-sties, food store with concrete floor, cow shed with space for 12 standings, open timber and tiled cattle shed, timber built and corrugated iron roof garage workshop, cart shed.

Chandlings Farmhouse and entrance in 1939.

Chandlings Farm, a dairy farm of approximately 77 acres, was owned by Christ Church college, and farmed by the Deane family from 1723, starting with Thomas Deane. The 1851 census shows a Thomas Deane aged 70 born on Chandlings Farm, with his wife, Elizabeth aged 58, and son, also Thomas, unmarried at age 30. In 1920 Ernest George Deane took over the farm from his father, Dennis Shepherd Deane. Ernest died in 1948 and Christ Church instigated a sale of the property. This was bought by the Revd Dugmore, who modernised the house. Some ten years later it was sold to Mr Lawson, who sold on to a hotelier, who eventually sold to a Lebanese millionaire, Farid Wakim, who extended it into a luxurious complex – Chandlings Manor – complete with thirty bedrooms, gymnasium, cinema, tennis courts, squash court and a rifle range. When resold in 1988 it was expected to reach £5 million. It was eventually purchased by Cothill School and is used as a private school to this day.

Chandlings Manor in 1988

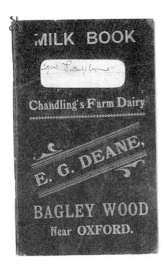

Cover of a Milk Book issued in 1942 by Mr E G Deane of Chandling's Farm Dairy to Mrs Smallbone who lived at Gibraltar House, Bagley Wood Road.

The Deane family of Chandlings Farm in 1934, in front of the cowshed. Reg Deane, Ernest Deane, Dick Deane, Violet Deane, John Deane with Tiger.

The dairy was started by Ernest Deane and supplied the surroundings villages. Ernest was in competition with Bill East, another local dairyman from Little London. He supplied the milk from his motorbike and sidecar, eventually purchasing a car then vans. The pint and quart glass bottles were all inscribed Chandlings Farm Dairy E G Deane.

Dairy delivery van from Chandlings Farm.

An attempt has been made to identify the earlier properties in Kennington, by comparing, within the Kelly's Directories, the names of occupants at different times. In 1925 there were 53 named private residents, mostly living at named properties. By 1939 numbers and road names had replaced these property names – but most can still be identified. Further investigation of property deeds could confirm these.

Original name	Occupant	Date	Occupant		Road	Date	New Name?
St Clara	Cripps	1925	Liversey	13	Bagley Wood	1939	
The Rosary	Walker	1925	Howes	38	Kenn. Rd	1939	
Ellenglade	Durbridge	1925	Jones	40	Kenn. Rd	1939	
Lynton	Draper	1925	Draper	44	Kenn. Rd	1939	
The Lawsons	Doman	1925	Merry	50	Kenn. Rd	1939	
The Bungalow	Ambler	1925	Ambler	54	Kenn. Rd	1939	
The Nook	Savage	1925	James	56	Kenn. Rd	1939	
Shirland	Pye	1925	Pye	64	Kenn. Rd	1939	Bermuda
Brockenhurst	Spracklen	1925	Spracklen	90	Kenn. Rd	1939	
Underwood	Smith	1925	Smith	92	Kenn. Rd	1939	
Fairfield	Thynne	1925	King	96	Kenn. Rd	1939	
Beaconsfield	Saunders	1925	Saunders	102	Kenn. Rd	1939	
Maybury	Granger	1925	Granger	108	Kenn. Rd	1939	
Woodside	Munday	1925	Munday	128	Kenn. Rd	1939	
	Kent	1925	Kent	170	Kenn. Rd	1939	
St Swithuns	Jones	1925	Jones	218	Kenn. Rd	1939	
	Acott	1925	Acott	83	Kenn. Rd	1939	
Stone House	Bishop	1925	Longthorp	105	Kenn. Rd	1939	
Polurrian	Rockall	1925	Rockall	107	Kenn. Rd	1939	
Belinda Cottage	Peedell	1925	Peedell	131	Kenn. Rd	1939	
Ingledene	Parker	1925	Mattingley	143	Kenn. Rd	1939	
The Hollies	Simkins	1925	Simkins	145	Kenn. Rd	1939	
The Hut	Silvester	1925	Wooldridge	149	Kenn. Rd	1939	
Thames View	Kimber	1925	Kimber	151	Kenn. Rd	1939	
The Hawthorns	King	1925	King	153	Kenn. Rd	1939	
Lowlands	Gibbons	1925	Gibbons	161	Kenn. Rd	1939	
Ava Cottage	Hewer	1925	Shayler	165	Kenn. Rd	1939	
Bryher	Robinson	1925	Peedell	167	Kenn. Rd	1939	
River View	Williams	1925	Burton	195	Kenn. Rd	1939	
The Lawn	Flower	1925	Barbour		Kenn. Rd	1939	
The Firs	Carter	1925	Carter	16	Kenville	1939	
Rose Villa	Allen	1925	Allen	2	Little London	1939	Woodbine Hse?
Copgrove Cott	Foster	1925	Blofeld	28	Little London	1939	
Copgrove	Farrer	1925	Farrer	30	Little London	1939	
Anglebee	Kirk	1925	Kirk	42	Little London	1939	Bagley Frith
Gibraltar House	Smallbone	1925	Smallbone	53	Little London	1939	
Greycote	Ellis	1925	Broomfield	63	Little London	1939	
The Mount	Mullins	1925	Mullins	143	Upper Road	1939	
Green Close	Gandy	1925	Gandy	192	Upper Road	1939	

Property names, and occupants, mentioned in 1925, but not recognised in later directories, include: Chennells occupying Castle Croft; Hicks at Dalbeathie; Covey at Glenlea; Mackenzie at Greenways; Spender at Halshanger; Faulkner at Haventhorpe; Phillips at Ingleside; Burton at Kenmore; Weeks at Lamorna; Penn at Nettleham and Herbert at Woodlands. Archibald Burton (at Kenmore in 1925) was at Riverview, 195 Kennington Road, by 1937. It is more than possible that this was the same property and had undergone a change of name.